# WHO WANTS TO BE A
# PIRATE?

## WHAT IT WAS REALLY LIKE
## IN THE GOLDEN AGE OF PIRACY

## BRIDGET HEOS

### illustrated by
## DANIEL DUNCAN

Henry Holt and Company
New York

# Avast, matey!

I can see by the sword in your hand and patch over your eye that you want to be a pirate

like
Captain Hook

or
Jack Sparrow

or
Long John Silver.

But those are fictional pirates. How would you like to be a real pirate from the Golden Age of Piracy? Like me, Captain Parrot! Climb aboard—I'll show you the difference between my day and a storybook day.

In a story, a pirate ship is
a frightening sight to behold.

In reality, it's not so much the sights that greet ye . . . as the smells! This ship is home to dozens of men—and their pets. Then there are the animals we eat—ducks, chickens, even a cow. We do have toilets, which open to the sea below. But the animals aren't exactly potty trained. I thank me lucky stars for the OCean breeze!

You may expect the captain's quarters
to be filled with fanciness and finery.

But in real life, my room is as humble as the rest of the ship, and me shipmates are welcome anytime. After all, if I start acting like a king, the men will elect a new captain. And I'll wind up marooned on an island!

# Time to get to work!

You didn't think piracy was all sword fighting
and swashbuckling, did ye?

Manning a ship is hard work—and it can be every bit as dangerous as a fight. See those sails way up high? A pirate must climb up to furl and unfurl them. One nasty lurch, and he'll fall to the deck. Tumbling into the water is no help. Most pirates can't swim!

Movies often show the danger of a storm
at sea. And that's true enough!

But though storms are treacherous, the doldrums can be even worse. On these warm, windless days, we drift aimlessly, far from loot and land. Our food supplies dwindle. To stave off hunger, we've even boiled and eaten our own boots!

Hark! A yonder ship! What treasures might it hold? Raise the black flag and prepare for battle! True, a sword fight is exciting. So are the cannonballs, pistols, and grenades!

You may think we force our captives to
walk the plank—but that's only in stories.

. . . but goods that we can use or sell:

cotton,

salted meat,

candles,

and fancy silk and velvet—perfect
for a new jacket. *Pirates do like to dress up!*

When the battle is won, we take the loot—
not the gold of lore . . .

But the aftermath is not so jolly. An injured arm or leg can lead to infection, putting a pirate in serious danger. No doctor on board? A carpenter will do, or anyone with a saw. There, now, good as gold.

In real life, we just throw them overboard.
However, not everyone we attack declares himself
an enemy. Many sailors turn pirate. On the merchant
ships we attack, captains can be cruel. They work
their men like dogs but feed them like birds.
Not on a pirate ship.

*At lunchtime, we feast!*

Come on!
Let's go!

Granted, even in times of plenty, our food isn't exactly fresh. Today we're having rancid pork, moldy bread, and wormy cheese. Ah well, raiders can't be choosers!

**Yo ho, yo ho.** Pirates really do like to have fun. We drink punch, dance, and have food fights. After all, we can always steal more from a passing ship.

Where to next? In stories, detailed maps
show where to find land—

and buried treasure.

But in reality, our maps aren't exactly accurate. They may be hundreds of miles off! So at night, when we think we're sailing smoothly, we may actually be approaching land.

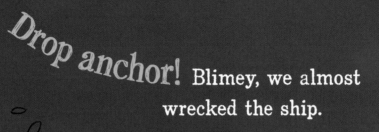

**Drop anchor!** Blimey, we almost wrecked the ship.

If we're lucky, the island will have fresh water
for our barrels and fresh fruit for our bellies.

Heave ho! No moldy biscuits tonight!

Eventually, we must find a port where we
can sell our loot and buy medicine and supplies.
In stories, pirates are hailed as heroes and
**always escape the law!**

But in real life, people don't care much for us.
My best option is to beg forgiveness and promise
never to go a-pirating again . . .

Then again, never say never!

Care to join us on our next **adventure?**

# Author's Note

Pirates have roamed the seas since ancient times, but they were especially common during the so-called Golden Age of Piracy, from 1650–1730. Captain Parrot is a fictional pirate, but he describes how things really were during this time.

Golden Age pirates made a living by robbing merchant ships crossing the sea (often in the Caribbean) and then selling the stolen goods. Many pirates had been merchant sailors themselves. As such, they were poorly paid and often badly treated—all while doing the dangerous work of manning a ship. Becoming a pirate was no less risky, but it did offer the prospect of better treatment and heartier meals. Much of the food was, of course, stolen from passing ships. Other times, it was gotten from islands—either deserted or home to Caribbean peoples.

Pirates were able to capture merchant ships because they greatly outnumbered the sailors onboard. This, along with the frightening reputation of the pirates, led many merchant ship captains to surrender rather than fight. The reputation was well-earned. Some pirates, such as Blackbeard, were unspeakably violent and cruel. Other pirates, however, had a code of decency that merchant ship captains did not. Many merchant captains engaged in slave trafficking, and while some pirates did, too, others would set any slaves they encountered free.

The Golden Age of Piracy came to an end when officials started cracking down on pirates. At first, colonial governors turned a blind eye to pirating because their colonies needed the goods being sold by pirates. As time went on, the colonies could attain the goods through legal channels, and so pirates were no longer needed. The military was ordered to pursue and capture pirates and bring them to trial. A pardon (like the one received by Captain Parrot) was rare. Convicted pirates were usually hanged, their bodies left dangling over the harbors—a warning to sailors not to follow in their footsteps.

# Bibliography

Cordingly, David. *Under the Black Flag*. New York: Random House, 1996.

Defoe, Daniel. *A General History of the Pyrates*. Columbia: University of South Carolina Press, 1972. Originally printed in 1724.*

*Pirates! Scourge of the Seven Seas*. Discovery Channel, 2011.

Rediker, Marcus. *Outlaws of the Atlantic*. Boston: Beacon Press, 2014.

Rediker, Marcus. *Villains of All Nations*. Boston: Beacon Press, 2004.

Stewart, David James. "'Rocks and Storms I'll Fear No More': Anglo-American Maritime Memorialization, 1700–1940." PhD Diss., Texas A&M University, 2004. nautarch.tamu.edu/Theses/pdf-files/Stewart-PhD2004.pdf

* The original book was titled *A General History of the Robberies and Murders of the Most Notorious Pyrates*. While the 1972 edition credits Defoe, the author of the 1724 edition is stated to be Captain Charles Johnson. Scholars believe this to be a pseudonym—possibly for Defoe, but perhaps for another author.

For Frankie Brewster
— B. H.

Henry Holt and Company, *Publishers since 1866*

Henry Holt® is a registered trademark of Macmillan Publishing Group, LLC

120 Broadway, New York, NY 10271 • mackids.com

Library of Congress Cataloging-in-Publication Data

Names: Heos, Bridget, author. | Duncan, Daniel, illustrator.

Title: Who wants to be a pirate? : what it was really like in the golden age of piracy / Bridget Heos ;

Illustrated by Daniel Duncan.

Description: First edition. | New York : Henry Holt and Company, 2019. | Includes bibliographical references.

Identifiers: LCCN 2019002035 | ISBN 9780805097702 (hardcover)

Subjects: LCSH: Pirates—History—17th century—Juvenile literature. | Pirates—History—18th century—

Juvenile literature. | Piracy—Caribbean Area—History—Juvenile literature. | Piracy—Atlantic Ocean Region—

History—Juvenile literature.

Classification: LCC G535 .H46 2019 | DDC 910.4/5—dc23

LC record available at https://lccn.loc.gov/2019002035

Our books may be purchased in bulk for promotional, educational, or business use.

Please contact your local bookseller or the Macmillan Corporate and Premium Sales Department at

(800) 221-7945 ext. 5442 or by email at MacmillanSpecialMarkets@macmillan.com.

First edition, 2019 / Designed by Vera Soki

The artist used a Wacom tablet and Photoshop to create the illustrations in this book.

Printed in China by Toppan Leefung Printing Ltd., Dongguan City, Guangdong Province

1  3  5  7  9  10  8  6  4  2